Primary Concepts®

Realia
Making Language Real

Designer: Hyru Gau

Editor: Kelly Stewart

©2007 Primary Concepts

P. O. Box 10043

Berkeley, CA 94709

www.primaryconcepts.com

ISBN 978-1-60184-058-5

Contents

Dear Teacher,

Primary Concepts has been collecting miniature objects for use in the classroom since 1984. At that time, its founders, Ruth Ingram and Ilsa Perse, mailed their first catalog of treasures for the classroom under the name Concepts to Go. Over the years, the Primary Concepts warehouse has grown to house over 5,000 objects. Teachers have learned to depend on Primary Concepts to provide the most appealing, realistic miniatures for language development, phonics concepts, and number work in both Spanish and English.

Keeping supplies of these small miniatures is no easy task, requiring the efforts of a full staff of specialists. We feel it is worth the effort, however, to provide teachers with these highly motivating, hands-on learning tools. When the company was in its first year of business, a teacher who saw our early math activity, Count-a-Pig, said, "These pigs make children want to count!" Just as the pigs motivate children to count, the thousands of other adorable objects (realia) make children want to talk, read, and spell.

Teachers use realia for a variety of oral language and vocabulary development activities: sorting, acting out stories and songs, and so on. With this guidebook, we have compiled our favorite language lessons for use with miniatures.

If you are new to the wonderful world of realia, this guidebook will offer our best tips for keeping your objects organized and ready for use in your lessons. Once you see how rich your daily language lessons become when you incorporate miniatures, you will wonder how you lived without them!

Sincerely,

Your Friends at Primary Concepts

Overview

Many children in today's classrooms struggle with the English language. Some come from homes where a foreign language is spoken; others simply have not developed a large enough academic vocabulary to thrive in the classroom. In either case, many children are at risk because of their limited English vocabularies.

Realia—miniature objects that resemble their real-world counterparts—provide an excellent tool to help these children develop essential English vocabulary. Realia enhance meaning and make vocabulary more concrete and, therefore, more comprehensible.

Collecting Realia

You may wish to purchase a collection of miniatures for language development from Primary Concepts or begin collecting your own. Good places to look are party stores, toy stores, craft supply stores, and fabric stores. Supplement the bought items with objects you can find around the house, such as a rock or a stone, a piece of wood, a nail, a screw, a paper clip, a button, a snap, and so on. The best objects are realistic and three-dimensional, and they need to be safe for classroom use (e.g., no sharp edges). Try to collect a variety of objects from these categories:

animals   kitchen play sets

dolls   sports equipment

doll clothing and accessories   tools

doll house furniture   toys

foods   vehicles

For a few activities, you will want to have a set of objects—such as frogs, cats, dogs, horses, snakes, or fish—in which each member of the set is slightly different. A set of fish, for example, could have different colors, shapes, sizes, textures, or patterns. These sets are good for language lessons in which children describe the differences among the individuals in the set.

Collecting realia can be a continuous pursuit. Once you have a basic collection, you may want to keep looking for more obscure items that would be useful in your teaching.

Getting Organized

Once you've gathered a collection of realia, your next step is to keep the miniatures organized so you can quickly find just the object you need. We find it best to keep the objects together in a Vocabulary Development Center, typically a storage compartment with drawers labeled by category. You can buy a storage compartment at a hardware store or purchase one from Primary Concepts. Put the objects in the organizer and label the drawers by category.

Using Realia

One of the main ways to use your Vocabulary Development Center is to prepare language learners for regular lessons in which their language deficits may pose a problem. For example, if you are reading a book that involves sea creatures or you are working on a science unit involving sea life, have the children who need extra language support identify the related sea creatures from your Vocabulary Development Center before you begin your lesson. Some teachers simply pass around the realia as the lesson is being taught. Using realia to preview or to review a lesson's vocabulary puts everyone on an equal footing and prepares all children for success.

In addition to this ongoing use of the Vocabulary Development Center, you can also use realia with small groups of children to build specific language skills. Such activities invite children to build their oral language by listening and speaking. Activities in this guidebook are focused on using language to compare, to describe, to differentiate, and to categorize. Children especially enjoy the storytelling activities.

As a general rule, when the children say a word or phrase incorrectly, simply repeat what they said using the correct word or phrase without comment. You might also want to expand on their verbalizations, transforming a word into a sentence or adding words to clarify meaning. For example, if a child says "seal," you might say, "I see a seal."

Prior Knowledge

Before you start working with a category of objects, check on the children's existing language skills so that you can build from those. Set out all of the sea creatures, for example, and have the children take turns pointing to an object and telling you one thing about it. Some children may be able to tell you the name of the object (e.g., "seal"); others may be able to impart some information about the object (e.g., "It swims."). Some children may be able to tell you the name of the object in their native language but not in English; others may not know the word in any language. You may wish to tape-record the session. Later, you can use the tape as a record of a child's progress.

Use the knowledge you gain from this activity to gear your language instruction to the needs of your class. It is best to work with groups of children whose language skills are at about the same level. The groups should be small (about 4–6 children) so that everyone will get plenty of talking time.

Assessing Progress

Since you will be working with the children in small groups, you will have a good understanding of their individual progress. Make sure that every child participates. Get into a routine of having each child repeat a word, a phrase, or a sentence so that everyone gets practice, even those who are most quiet. Keep a running record of observations, especially individual needs that are best addressed separately, such as articulation problems or attention issues that may be getting in the way of progress.

Periodically, assess children's progress by setting out the same group of objects you used to assess their prior knowledge and ask them again to tell you about the objects. Listen together to the audiotape of the child's first verbalizations. It will undoubtedly be clear to you as well as to the child how much progress has been made towards fluency with the language.

Additional Materials

Besides the objects, you will find the following materials useful in teaching the activities.

Sorting Mats and Label Cards

You can purchase sorting mats from Primary Concepts or make ones using the blackline masters on pages 49–52. You can make label cards by copying page 53 on cardstock, laminating the sheet, and then cutting out the cards. Children can use the label cards on the sorting mats.

Felt Workmats

A workmat can be useful in keeping children focused on the activity task. Sheets of colorful felt work especially well.

Baskets or Trays

Baskets or trays make convenient places to put the objects that the children will be sorting and using for storytelling.

Story Mats

Story mats provide an environment on which children can use miniatures to act out stories. The mats can be made by cutting out pieces of felt using the templates on pages 55–62. A good size for individual story mats is about 9" by 12". If you are artistic, you may wish to design your own environments. On the following page, you will find examples of the different kinds of story mats you may wish to use.

Story Mat Scenes

At the Pond (page 55)

Realia:
forest animals (e.g., frog, rabbit, duck, fox, owl, bird, skunk, bear, deer), nest, boat, picnic basket, blanket

Picnic in the Park (page 59)

Realia:
skateboard, kite, camera, food (e.g., apple, grapes, pizza, cake), ball, family (e.g., mother, father, sister, brother)

Under the Sea (page 56)

Realia:
sea creatures (e.g., shark, octopus, starfish, crab, turtle, lobster), sunken ship, treasure chest

Barnyard (page 60)

Realia:
farm animals (e.g., cow, horse, sheep, pig, hen, goat, goose, rooster, turkey, donkey, cat, dog), wagon

In the Jungle (page 57)

Realia:
rainforest animals (e.g., monkey, parrot, tiger, crocodile, butterfly), log

Around Town (page 61)

Realia:
cars, airplane, helicopter, bus, motorcycle, bicycle, truck, signs

Bug Life (page 58)

Realia:
ladybug, spider, butterfly, bee, fly, ant, worm, snail

African Adventure (page 62)

Realia:
lion, elephant, zebra, hippo, jeep, rocks

I Spy

To get started, play a game of I Spy.

SET UP   Spread out about five different objects on a felt workmat. Pick objects from one category, such as Zoo Animals.

ACTIVITY   Choose a secret object to describe, and give the children a clue. The children should be able to name the object from your description. For example, using Zoo Animals, here are some possible clues:

- I spy an animal with a long neck. (giraffe)
- I spy an animal that looks like a horse with stripes. (zebra)
- I spy an animal that lives in a cold place. (polar bear)
- I spy an animal with very big ears. (elephant)

When a child identifies the correct animal, have the child say the word and its description in a sentence. "A giraffe has a long neck." Then have everyone say the sentence in unison.

You can repeat this activity many times with different sets of objects.

EXTENSION   Once the children are familiar with the activity, have them think of I Spy clues for the others to identify.

Pass It On

In this activity, everyone gets a chance to say something about an object.

SET UP   Put a few miniatures in a paper bag. Have the children sit in a circle.

ACTIVITY   Pick an object from the bag, and hold it up. Say one thing about the object using a complete sentence. Then pass the object to the child sitting next to you, and have that child say something new about the object. Continue around the circle in this manner. Here are examples of possible statements for a carrot:

- You can eat carrots.
- Carrots are orange.
- Carrots grow in the ground.
- Rabbits like carrots.
- This carrot is small.

After each child says a sentence, repeat the sentence aloud, correcting it or clarifying it as necessary. A child might say, "You eats carrots." You would say, "You eat carrots." Then have the whole group repeat the sentence.

After the object has gone around the circle, let a child pick a new object and repeat the activity.

EXTENSION   Next time you meet with the group, choose a different set of objects for Pass It On.

Round Robin Sentences

The miniatures coax the children to talk in sentences in this activity.

SET UP   You will need the entire Vocabulary Development Center filled with objects.

ACTIVITY   Choose an object from a drawer of your Vocabulary Development Center. Put it on the table, and say, "I see a (name of object)." Then choose an object from a different drawer, and give it to a child. Invite the child to make up a sentence that includes both words (e.g., *pig* and *apple*).

Now take an object from another drawer, and give it to another child. Have the child make up a sentence with this object and the first object. Keep going this way until everyone has had a turn. Here is an example:

- (pig)   I see a <u>pig</u>.
- (apple)   The <u>pig</u> ate an <u>apple</u>.
- (boat)   The <u>pig</u> jumped into a <u>boat</u>.
- (hat)   The <u>pig</u> is wearing a <u>hat</u>.
- (cat)   The <u>pig</u> ran after a <u>cat</u>.

EXTENSION   Write each sentence on chart paper, and have the children read each one.

Old MacDonald

Use this familiar song for identifying farm animals and animal noises.

SET UP Set out farm animals on a felt workmat for all the children to see.

ACTIVITY Sing "Old MacDonald" together naming a new animal for each verse. Have the children take turns finding the animal and saying the animal sound.

Old MacDonald had a farm, E-I-E-I-O.

And on that farm, he had a pig, E-I-E-I-O.

With an oink-oink here and an oink-oink there.

Here an oink, there an oink,

Everywhere an oink-oink.

Old MacDonald had a farm, E-I-E-I-O.

EXTENSION On another day, use realia to act out the verses of "The Farmer and the Dell." For this song, you will need a farmer, his wife, a child, a nurse, a cow, a dog, a cat, a rat, and a piece of cheese. Add each character to the felt workmat for each new verse, until the end when the cheese "stands alone."

The farmer in the dell, the farmer in the dell,
Heigh-ho, the derry-o, the farmer in the dell.

The farmer takes a wife, the farmer takes a wife,
Heigh-ho, the derry-o, the farmer takes a wife.

The wife takes a child, the wife takes a child,
Heigh-ho, the derry-o, the wife takes a child.

[Continue with verses for a nurse, a cow, a dog, a cat, a rat, and the cheese.]

The cheese stands alone, the cheese stands alone,
Heigh-ho, the derry-o, the cheese stands alone.

The Enormous Carrot

Children enjoy retelling this variation of a familiar folktale.

SET UP   You will need a carrot, a farmer, a wife, a child, a cow, a horse, a dog, a cat, and a mouse. Put the objects in a basket. Set out a felt workmat.

ACTIVITY   Tell the story of "The Enormous Carrot." As you do, have the children find each item you name and put it on the workmat.

> Once upon a time, a farmer planted a carrot seed in his garden. He watered the plant every day and soon the plant grew and grew. One day, he decided the carrot was ready to eat. He pulled and pulled, but the carrot would not come up. So the farmer called for his wife to help him. The wife pulled on the farmer, and the farmer pulled on the carrot. They pulled and pulled, but the carrot would not come up.
>
> So the farmer called for the cow to help. The cow pulled on the wife, the wife pulled on the farmer, and the farmer pulled on the carrot. They pulled and pulled, but the carrot would not come up.
>
> [Continue the story with the farmer calling the horse, the dog, and the cat for help.]
>
> So the farmer called for a mouse to help. The mouse pulled on the cat, the cat pulled on the dog, the dog pulled on the horse, the horse pulled on the cow, the cow pulled on the wife, the wife pulled on the farmer, and the farmer pulled on the carrot. They pulled and pulled, and the carrot finally came up.

EXTENSION   When you have finished the story, ask the children what happened *first*, *next*, and *last*.

Henny Penny

Did the sky really fall?

SET UP You will need the following objects: a hen for Henny Penny, a rooster for Cocky Locky, a duck for Ducky Lucky, a goose for Goosey Loosey, a turkey for Turkey Lurkey, a fox for Foxy Loxy, and a small acorn or other nut.

ACTIVITY Have the children act out the story of "Henny Penny" as you tell it. Drop an acorn or other nut on Henny Penny's head at the start of the story.

> Henny Penny was walking in the barnyard one day. Something hit her on the head. "The sky is falling," she said. "I must go and tell the king."
>
> On the way, she met Cocky Locky. "Where are you going?" asked Cocky Locky. "The sky is falling. I must tell the king," said Henny Penny. Cocky Locky decided to come, too. So Henny Penny and Cocky Locky set off to see the king.
>
> A little farther on, they met Ducky Lucky. "Where are you going?" asked Ducky Lucky. "The sky is falling. We are going to tell the king," said Henny Penny. Ducky Lucky decided to come, too. So Henny Penny, Cocky Locky, and Ducky Lucky set off to see the king.
>
> [Continue in a similar way with Goosey Loosey and Turkey Lurkey.]
>
>
> A little later, they met Foxy Loxy. "Where are you going?" asked Foxy Loxy. "The sky is falling. We are going to tell the king," said Henny Penny.
>
> But Foxy Loxy told Henny Penny that he knew a better way to get to the king. So Henny Penny, Cocky Locky, Ducky Lucky, Goosey Loosey, and Turkey Lurkey followed Foxy Loxy.
>
> Soon they came to a dark hole. Foxy Loxy said to go inside. First Turkey Lurkey went in. Then Goosey Loosey went in. Then Ducky Lucky went in. Then Cocky Locky went in. Then Henny Penny heard them say, "Run home, Henny Penny!" And she did.

EXTENSION Invite the children to act out the story on their own. Before they get started, ask them to tell you what happened at the beginning, the middle, and the end of the story.

Ten in the Bed

Here's another familiar song that can be acted out with realia.

SET UP Put ten different animals on a "bed," either a copy of the Ten in the Bed blackline master on page 46 or a piece of cloth to suggest a bed.

ACTIVITY Sing the song "Ten in the Bed" together, and have the children take turns acting out each verse. Each child should find the smallest animal to fall off the bed.

There were ten in the bed,

And the little one said, "Roll over. Roll over."

They all rolled over, and one fell out.

There were nine in the bed,

And the little one said, "Roll over. Roll over."

They all rolled over, and one fell out.

[Continue in a similar way with eight, seven, six, five, four, three, and two in bed.]

There was one in the bed,

And that one said, "Good night!"

EXTENSION Have the children sing and act out the song on their own.

All or None

Words like *all*, *none*, *any*, and *some* are tricky for young children.

SET UP Make a copy of the Ten in the Bed blackline master on page 46, and gather 12 miniature animals.

ACTIVITY Use words from the list below in sentences.

all	some	none	most	more
few	many	less	more	any

Ask a child to show the meaning of the sentence. For example, if you say, "A few animals are on the bed," the child might put three animals on the bed. When the child has completed the task, talk about what the child has done. For example, say, "Are *any* animals on the bed? Are *all* the animals on the bed?" Make sure the children understand that most of these words are not exact, so there are a variety of ways to show the meaning of a sentence.

Here are some sample sentences:

- *All* the animals are on the bed.
- *Some* of the animals are on the bed.
- *None* of the animals are on the bed.
- *Most* of the animals are on the bed.
- *More* animals are on the bed than off the bed.
- *Fewer* animals are on the bed than off the bed.
- *Many* animals are on the bed, but a *few* are off the bed.
- A *dozen* animals are on the bed.
- A *couple* animals are on the bed.
- *Less than* five animals are on the bed.
- *More than* five animals are on the bed.

EXTENSION Repeat the activity on another day with a different scene and objects. For example, you could use the At the Pond story mat on page 55 and talk about animals either in or out of the pond.

Color Words

The children identify basic color words in this activity.

SET UP   Set out objects with readily identifiable colors, such as an apple, a strawberry, a wagon, a cucumber, peas, a green pepper, a banana, a lemon, a piece of cheese, a chick, a school bus, an orange, a carrot, a pig, grapes, a polar bear, a sheep, an elephant, a hippo, and so on.

ACTIVITY   Introduce one color at a time. Name the color, and have the children look for objects that share that color. For yellow, for example, the children might identify things like a banana, a lemon, a piece of cheese, a chick, and a school bus. For each object, have the children say the sentence, "The (name of object) is yellow." Ask the children if they can name other things that have that color.

Then talk about how the color appears different in the objects that share a color. Children might notice, for example, that the chick is *darker than* the cheese. Conversely, the cheese is *lighter than* the chick.

Repeat the activity with each of the different colors.

EXTENSION   Show the children objects with more than one color, and have them describe each object. A child might say, for example, "A zebra is black and white striped." or "The bunny is white with a pink nose." Objects might include those with stripes (e.g., zebra, tiger, bee, snake, flag), those with dots (e.g., ladybug, spider, snake), as well as other multicolored objects, such as a parrot.

Mary Wore Her Red Dress

This song helps children learn clothing and color words.

SET UP Set out objects from the Clothes category, plus other things to wear such as glasses, a hat, a ring, a shoe, and so on. Make copies of the Paper Doll blackline master on page 47.

ACTIVITY Together with the children, sing the song "Mary Wore Her Red Dress." For each verse, hold up something Mary might wear. Put it on the paper doll. Have the children identify the color, name the clothing, and then sing the verse using those words.

Mary wore her yellow socks, yellow socks, yellow socks,
Mary wore her yellow socks, all day long.

EXTENSION Pass out copies of the Paper Doll blackline master, and have the children draw clothing on the template. When they are finished, ask a volunteer to share what they drew and to name their paper doll. Then everyone can sing about the child's doll. Here's an example:

James wore his brown pants, brown pants, brown pants,
James wore his brown pants, all day long.

James wore a red hat, red hat, red hat,
James wore a red hat, all day long.

The Language of Shapes

Shapes are everywhere in the world around us.

SET UP Gather together the objects in the list below and others that have the basic shapes of a circle, a triangle, a rectangle, an oval, a square, or a diamond. Copy the Label Cards blackline master on page 53 and cut out the cards for the shapes.

circle	triangle	rectangle	oval	square	diamond
hat	pizza piece	map	skateboard	block	kite
snap	cheese	dollar bill	bread	table	
coins	sail	book	tennis racket		
lock	cone	rug	spoon		
plate		placemat			
cake		stamp			
drum		flag			
yo-yo					
wheels					
clock					

ACTIVITY Introduce one shape at a time. Name the shape, and have the children look for objects that have that shape. For a circle, for example, the children might identify things like a coin, the top of a hat, and so on.

Repeat the activity with each of the different shapes. Then look for objects that have more than one of the shapes. For example, the children might notice an oval on the face of a dollar bill.

EXTENSION Compare the shapes with questions like the following:

- How many sides does a triangle have? a rectangle? a circle?
- In which shape are all the sides the same length?
- How is an oval like a circle? How is it different?

Sounds in Words

For many children, especially English-language learners, certain sounds in words are difficult to distinguish. In this activity, children find objects for words, such as *map* and *mop*, that differ in only one sound.

SET UP   Find pairs of objects like the following that differ in only one sound:

map/mop	cat/coat/kite	bread/bed
bat/boat/boot	lamb/lamp	black/block
bear/pear	socks/six	three/tree
ship/sheep	lock/log	

Mix them up, and place them on the table where everyone can see them.

ACTIVITY   Name an object, and have the children find it. Note when a child is confused by a similar sounding word, *map* instead of *mop*, for example.

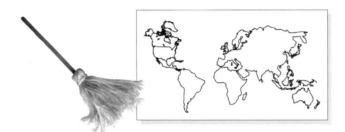

EXTENSION   Invite a child to name an object, and have the other children locate it. Encourage the child to articulate clearly so the other children can find the correct object.

See It, Say It

In this activity, the children must listen carefully to see whether the word is pronounced correctly.

SET UP Set out some objects such as those listed below on a felt workmat.

ACTIVITY Name an object, either pronouncing the word correctly or incorrectly. Have the children point to the object only if you have said its name correctly. For example, if the object on the table is a horse and you say "hearse," the children should not point to the horse. Mix up times when you say the actual word and when you make a miscue.

Object	Miscue
horse	hearse
lion	line
watch	wash
lock	look
clock	clack
worm	warm
saw	song
peas	peace
truck	trunk
bird	board
ring	wing
log	long
fox	fax

EXTENSION Let the children take turns being the one to say a word. If the child says the word correctly, the other children point to the object.

Sort and Say

Introduce sorting with this basic category sorting activity.

SET UP   Set up one or more sorting stations. At each station, provide a sorting mat (see pages 49–52) and objects from three or four categories. Mix up the objects and spread them on the table.

ACTIVITY   Have the children work in pairs to sort the objects into categories. Encourage them to discuss with each other what the categories might be and what objects go in each. Ask questions like the following as they work:

- What is this group (point to a group) called?
- Why is the (name of object) in this group?
- What other things could go in this group?

When the children are finished, help them name the categories. Label the columns on the sorting mat with the category names. Then have the children say the objects in each category using sentence patterns. Say together, for example, "An orange is a fruit. A strawberry is a fruit."

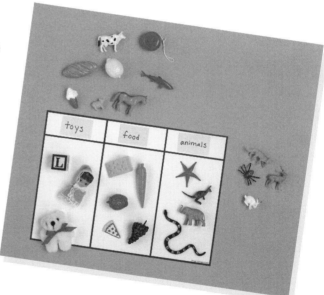

EXTENSION   Write the sentences on chart paper, and then read the sentences aloud.

Category

Build language using an old favorite game.

SET UP Choose a category, such as Zoo Animals, Food, or Toys. Put the objects for that category on a felt workmat where everyone can see them.

ACTIVITY Play the game Category with the children. For example, for the category Zoo Animals, clap and say, "Category (clap, clap), zoo animals (clap, clap), elephant (clap, clap), giraffe (clap, clap), zebra (clap, clap)," and so on. Pick up the animal you name. Keep the pace brisk and fun.

Then play Category again with the children. This time go around the group and have each child name an example and pick up the object as he says its name.

Repeat with other categories on different days.

EXTENSION Invite the children to name examples of the category that are not on the workmat.

Go Togethers

A sock and a shoe go together. A needle and thread go together. But how do a car and a skate go together?

SET UP Set out a large number of miniatures from a variety of categories on a felt workmat.

ACTIVITY Take two objects that are alike in some way and show them to the children. Ask the children to tell you how they are alike. Here are some examples:

- a car and a skate (Both have four wheels.)
- a snake and a worm (Both have no legs.)
- a watch and a clock (Both tell time.)
- a map and a globe (Both show places in the world.)

EXTENSION Now invite the children to find pairs of objects that are alike in some way and tell how they are alike.

Land, Sea, or Sky

Children sort objects by place (i.e., land, sea, or sky) in this activity.

SET UP   You'll need a copy of the three-column Sorting Mat from page 50 labeled "sky," "land," and "sea," plus objects such as those listed below. Label cards can be found on page 53.

sky	land	sea
airplane	bus	boat
helicopter	car	shark
bird	motorcycle	seal
butterfly	train	whale
kite	bicycle	dolphin
	truck	octopus

ACTIVITY   Work with the children to sort the objects. Have a child put an object on the sorting mat and tell why the object goes there. Ask the child if the object could go in more than one category. An airplane, for example, does "land," even though it is designed to fly in the sky.

EXTENSION   Use different animals for this sorting activity: zoo animals, farm animals, forest animals, sea creatures, and pets. Children can sort the objects on a copy of a five-column Sorting Mat (see page 52) or in the drawers in which the objects are stored. Labels can be found on page 53. Talk about how some animals can be found in more than one place.

Secret Sort

Can the children figure out the secret sorting rule?

SET UP   Set up a two-column Sorting Mat (see page 49) with one column labeled "yes" and one column labeled "no." Label cards can be found on page 53. Place miscellaneous objects near the mat.

ACTIVITY   Pick a sorting rule, such as animals with four legs, things you can eat, things that fly, or things that are orange. Tell the children to watch closely as you sort objects on the mat. Ask the children to figure out how you are sorting the objects. Take objects one at a time and put them in either the "yes" or "no" column according to your sorting rule. For example, if your secret sorting rule is things that fly, you would put a bee in the "yes" column, a fox in the "no" column, a kite in the "yes" column, a sled in the "no" column, and so on.

After you have a few items sorted, ask the children if they think they know the sorting rule. Then call on individual children to tell what they think the sorting rule might be and why. If a child is incorrect, continue sorting, putting objects in the "yes" and "no" columns. Again, invite the children to guess the sorting rule and tell why.

When a correct sorting rule is named, have the children complete the sorting with the remaining unsorted objects. Summarize by saying, for example, "All the things in the 'yes' column can fly. None of the things in the 'no' column can fly." Have the children repeat a sentence for each object (e.g., "The bee can fly. A fox cannot fly.").

EXTENSION   Repeat the activity with other secret sorts. After the children are familiar with the activity, let the children take turns being the teacher with the secret sort.

Same and Different

With this activity, the children focus on finer distinctions.

SET UP   Use a set of the same type of animal, but have each individual animal in the set differ in some way from the others. The sets could be spiders, snakes, fish, horses, frogs, dogs, or cats.

ACTIVITY   Pick two objects at random and ask a child to tell how those two objects are alike and how they are different. For example, they might say the following:

- One fish is red. The other fish is blue.
- Both fish have fins.
- The blue fish has a long nose. The red fish doesn't.
- The tails are different shapes.

Continue with other pairs of the same kind of object.

EXTENSION   On another day, focus on a different type of animal.

By the Numbers

How many legs does a chicken have? How about a turtle? a snake?

SET UP Use a copy of the five-column Sorting Mat (see page 52) labeled with the numbers 0, 2, 4, 6, and 8. Display the animals listed below.

0	2	4	6	8
snake	bird	rabbit	ant	spider
worm	hen	deer	ladybug	octopus
fish	man	turtle	fly	
snail	monkey	horse	butterfly	

ACTIVITY Invite the children to sort the animals by number of legs (arms or appendages). As you work together to sort the objects, be sure to engage the children in conversation about the animals.

- Which have six legs?
- What do we call these kinds of animals? (insects)
- Which have zero legs? How do they move?

EXTENSION Use vehicles and a copy of the four-column Sorting Mat on page 51. Invite the children to sort the vehicles by the number of wheels they have.

0	2	4	More than 4
boat	airplane	wagon	truck
sled	motorcycle	car	bus
	bike		train

Shelf Sort

In this activity, children sort objects on store shelves. Which things go together on a shelf?

SET UP   Make four or more copies of the Store Shelves blackline master on page 48. Near each mat, place a basket of objects indicating a different kind of store.

> **Grocery Store**: fruits, vegetables, other types of foods
>
> **Toy and Sports Store**: sports gear, toys, dolls
>
> **Apparel Store**: clothing and accessories
>
> **Kitchen Store**: utensils, silverware, place settings, pots and pans
>
> **Hardware Store**: tools, lock, key, garden equipment

ACTIVITY   Tell the children to imagine they are store clerks and they need to organize their merchandise on shelves. Have the children work in pairs to do their sorting. Tell them that there is no one right answer to the sorting.

When the children have completed their sorting, have them tell you how they sorted the items. How are all the items on each shelf alike? Talk about what you would find on the *top*, *middle*, and *bottom* shelves.

EXTENSION   Have the children move to another "store" for a different kind of sorting. Continue this way until everyone has been to each store.

Words for Money

A penny is easy to recognize because of its color. The quarter is largest. But which coin is the dime, and which is the nickel?

SET UP Give each child a magnifying glass and a coin (i.e., penny, nickel, dime, or quarter) to examine. Put the coins on a felt workmat.

ACTIVITY Name a coin, and ask children to find it on the felt workmat. After all four coins have been identified, turn them all over and say the coin names again. Can the children identify the coins, both heads and tails?

Then ask each child to examine a coin closely, preferably with a magnifying glass. Go around the group having each child tell about his or her coin. Do the other coins look the same or different? In what ways?

Explain that the "head" side is called "heads" and the reverse side is called "tails." Have the children flip their coins. How many come up heads? How many are tails?

EXTENSION Tell the children how much each coin is worth. Then put the coins in order of value. Which coin has the greatest value? Is it the largest coin? Which coin has the least value? Is it the smallest coin? Note that the smallest coin—the dime—is worth more than both the nickel and the penny.

At the Store

In this activity, children pretend to be customers and clerks at a store.

SET UP Use copies of the Store Shelves from page 48. Place objects on the Store Shelves. Here are some examples:

Grocery Store: fruits, vegetables, other types of foods

Toy and Sports Store: sports gear, toys, dolls

Apparel Store: clothing and accessories

Kitchen Store: utensils, silverware, place settings, pots and pans

Hardware Store: tools, lock, key, garden equipment

ACTIVITY Have the children work in pairs. One is the store clerk, and one is a customer. Here are some talking points:

- The clerk welcomes the customer.
- The clerk tells the customer about the different items in the store.
- The customer asks questions about the different items.
- The customer asks about prices for items of interest.
- The clerk compares the items in the store and their prices.
- The customer selects an item to buy from the store and explains why.
- The customer pretends to give the clerk money for the purchase.
- The clerk pretends to give the customer change.
- The customer and clerk thank each other and say good-bye.

EXTENSION You may wish to provide price tags for the different items. Then children can use play money to act out paying for the merchandise.

From Head to Toe

Do your children know words for the parts of the body? Use this activity to find out.

SET UP Give each child a different doll.

ACTIVITY Play a game of Simon Says with the children using parts of the body on the dolls. In the game of Simon Says, children are supposed to do what they are instructed only if you say, "Simon says." Here are some examples:

- Simon says, "Point to the nose."
- Simon says, "Touch the toes."
- Simon says, "Find the chin."
- Now, point to the elbow.

Try to use all the body parts listed below in your game of Simon Says.

ankle	eyes	hands	nose
arms	face	head	shoulders
cheeks	feet	hip	thumb
chin	fingers	knees	toes
ears	forehead	legs	waist
elbow	hair	mouth	wrist
eyebrows			

EXTENSION Make a transparency of the Paper Doll blackline master on page 47. Display the transparency on the overhead projector. Draw eyes, hair, eyebrows, mouth, nose, and so on on the transparency. Invite the children to name the body parts.

People Dolls

In this activity, the children are encouraged to use words to describe people, body parts, clothes, colors, and so on.

SET UP   Display different dolls.

ACTIVITY   Start with one of the dolls. Pass the doll from child to child, having each child say one new thing about the doll. Continue until no one can think of anything else to say about the doll.

- This is a man.
- The man has a blue shirt.
- The man has black shoes.
- The man has brown pants.
- The man has black hair.
- The man is wearing a black belt.
- The pants have pockets.
- The blue shirt has a collar.
- The blue shirt has five buttons.

EXTENSION   For an added language challenge, invite the children to give a cumulative response. Each child in turn must say each thing that the previous person has said plus one more thing. So for the man above, the last child would say the following:

This is a man with black hair who is wearing black shoes, a black belt, brown pants with pockets, and a blue shirt with a collar and five buttons.

All in the Family

Words for family relationships are often difficult for young children.

SET UP Again, set out all the dolls. You'll need female and male dolls of various ages.

ACTIVITY Tell the children that you are going to describe two or more of the dolls. They need to listen carefully and find the dolls you are describing. For example, ask children to find the following:

- a boy and his sister
- a girl and her mother
- a grandmother and a granddaughter
- a mother and her father
- a young man and his wife

Use words for the relationships between the family members. Here are some words to be sure to use:

boy	girl	woman	man
sister	brother	wife	husband
mother	father	daughter	son
grandmother	grandfather	granddaughter	grandson
aunt	uncle	niece	nephew

EXTENSION Put all the dolls in a paper bag. Pass around the bag, having the children take turns picking out two dolls and telling how they could be related.

Where, Oh Where?

The dog is on the couch. The cat is under the table. Where is the mouse?

SET UP Put some objects in a basket, for example, a bowl, a spoon, a fork, a knife, a plate, and a placemat. You may wish to combine objects with a related felt story mat. (See the suggestions on pages 55–62.) For example, you might use the blanket, the plate, the fork, the spoon, the knife, and the pizza with the Picnic in the Park story mat.

ACTIVITY Give directions for the children to follow. Use prepositions to describe where things should go. Have the children take turns following your directions. Here is an example:

- Put the bowl on the plate.
- Put the spoon beside the plate.
- Put the fork on the other side of the plate.
- Put the knife between the spoon and the plate.
- Put the spoon in the bowl.
- Put the placemat under the plate.
- Take the bowl off the plate.

On another day, use a different group of objects, and give different directions using words to describe where the objects go. Try to include the following prepositions:

in	on	under	out	over	by
between	above	below	around	off	beside
inside	outside	up	down	through	with
in front of	behind	into	across		

EXTENSION Invite the children to give directions for classmates to follow.

Details, Details

Children use descriptive words and prepositional phrases to describe objects and their location in a scene.

SET UP Use felt story mats and related objects. (See pages 55–62.) Set up a scene on each story mat.

ACTIVITY Display one story mat at a time. Invite a child to describe what they see. Here is an example:

> I see a duck in a pond. A green frog is beside a rock by the pond. A goat is in a row boat….

When the child is finished, ask the other children if there are any details they would like to add.

EXTENSION Set out a story mat and place the objects in a basket nearby. Tell the children where to put the objects on the mat to create a scene.

Barrier Game

With this game, children get feedback about how clear their descriptions are.

SET UP You will need pairs of story mats and pairs of matching objects for this activity. (See pages 55–62.) Children will also need some kind of barrier, for example, a large book.

ACTIVITY Have the children work in pairs, each with a matching story mat and objects. If the two sit side by side, they will be able to compare story mats more easily than if they sit face to face. Place a barrier between the two so that they cannot see each other's story mats.

Explain the barrier game: One child starts by putting objects on his story mat and telling the other child what and where he put the object. The other child tries to place the same object in the same location on her story mat. Once the object is placed, they remove the barrier and compare story mats. Were the directions clear? What differences are there and why?

The game continues with the second child putting an object on her story mat and describing it for the first child.

EXTENSION Invite the child who is the "describer" to look at the other child's story mat. If the object is not in the same place as it is on his mat, he can give more information. For example, if the first child says, "I put a bird in the tree," he might add detail by saying, "I put the bird in the top of the tree."

All in a Row

Who is first in line? Who is last?

SET UP Choose a set of animals and line them up in a row, all pointing one direction. You might use an object for the animals to be headed towards, such as a boat.

ACTIVITY Tell the children that you are going to describe where an animal is in line and they are to tell you which one it is. Here are some examples:

- It is *first* in line.
- It is *last* in line.
- It is the *second* (*third*, *fourth*, *fifth*) in line.
- It is *between* the horse and the pig.
- It is next *after* the cow.
- It comes just *before* the goat.
- It is *closest* to the boat.
- It is *farthest* from the boat.

Set up a different row of objects on a different day, and invite the children to take turns giving clues. Use position words like the following:

| first | next | last | before | after | |
| closest | farthest | second | third | fourth | fifth |

EXTENSION Add more animals to the row. Tell the children where to place each new addition. For example, ask a child to put a dog between the tiger and the elephant.

What Do You Do?

Children use lots of verbs in this activity.

SET UP   Set out the objects listed below.

ACTIVITY   Ask the children to pick an item and tell what they might do with it. For example, a child who picks a shovel might say, "You dig with a shovel." Make sure the children use complete sentences and that they use the proper English preposition following the verb, if necessary. Typical responses are listed below, although many others are just as correct.

Object	Verb	Object	Verb
car	drive	pencil	write with
horse	ride on	ring	wear
shovel	dig with	couch	sit on
tree	climb	football	catch or throw
bed	sleep in	broom	sweep with
book	read	lamp	turn on
straw	drink with	banana	peel, eat
camera	take pictures with	drum	beat
television	watch	guitar	play
kite	fly	phone	talk on
knife	cut with	flag	wave
radio	listen to	pan	fry in
whistle	blow	cake	bake
crayon	color with		

EXTENSION   Have the children pick a secret item and pantomime what they would do with it. For a whistle, for example, a child would pretend to blow a whistle. The other children find the item the child has picked and tell what the child is doing. "Megan is blowing a whistle."

How Does It Move?

A horse trots. A frog jumps. A fish swims. A bird flies.

SET UP To each child, hand out an animal, such as a rabbit, a deer, a bird, a spider, a fish, a snake, a horse, a frog, an owl, a shark, a worm, a fox, or a crab.

ACTIVITY Have each child show you and then tell you how her animal moves. For example, a child with a rabbit would show you how a rabbit can hop, run, and walk. A child with a horse might show you how the horse can trot, jump, run, and prance. A child with a bird might show how the bird can fly, soar in the air, and hop on the ground. Help the children with the words they need to describe the actions.

EXTENSION Have the children identify other animals that move in the same way. For example, a child might say that a worm slides like a snake, a crab crawls like a spider, or a frog hops like a rabbit.

Meaning What?

This activity is intended to build awareness that a word may have more than one meaning.

SET UP Display miniatures for words that have more than one meaning. Here are some examples:

bat	orange	pear	saw	fly	straw
glasses	watch	horse	duck	bee	ball
club	bowl	ring	stamp	snap	

ACTIVITY Say sentences like the following, and have the children identify the object that represents a word you are using in the sentence but that also has a different meaning. Then talk with the children about the two ways you might use the same word. Here are some examples:

- I saw a <u>bat</u> flying in the barn. (baseball bat)
- A bird can <u>fly</u>. (the insect fly)
- Put the <u>glasses</u> in the dishwasher when they are dirty. (glasses to read)
- <u>Watch</u> out for the dog. (a watch that tells time)
- Give the sheep some <u>straw</u>. (a straw you use for drinking)
- I have a <u>pair</u> of green socks. (a pear you eat)
- I'm <u>hoarse</u> from talking too much. (a horse)
- She had to <u>duck</u> to get into the playhouse. (a duck that swims)
- Will you <u>be</u> my friend? (a buzzing bee)
- Cinderella went to the <u>ball</u>. (a bouncing ball)
- I belong to a <u>club</u>. (a golf club)
- My family likes to go <u>bowl</u>ing. (a bowl for cereal)
- The bells <u>ring</u> every morning. (a ring on your finger)
- <u>Stamp</u> your feet if you are cold. (a stamp on an envelope)
- The shirt was <u>orange</u> with black spots. (an orange you eat)
- I <u>saw</u> my dad. (a <u>saw</u> to cut wood)
- <u>Snap</u> your fingers. (a snap on clothes)

EXTENSION Now invite the children to choose an object and make up a sentence using another meaning of the word.

Long and Short

Words are interesting. Some get shortened in common usage. Others get combined to form compound words.

SET UP Set out objects such as these that can be said in two ways:

telephone (phone)   television (TV)   airplane (plane)

bicycle (bike)   hippopotamus (hippo)   mother (mom)

father (dad)   saxophone (sax)

ACTIVITY Have the children name two words, one long and one short, for each object.

EXTENSION Introduce compound words. Mix up pairs of objects that combine to make compound words, and display them on the table. Have the children find the pairs of objects, say the compound word, and use it in a sentence. Here are some examples:

- cow + boy
- horse + shoe
- pan + cake
- book + worm
- pig + pen
- star + fish
- lady + bug
- drum + stick
- basket + ball
- cup + cake
- bed + time (clock)
- straw + berry

Big and Little

Which one is bigger? Which one is smaller? Which one is biggest of all?

SET UP You will need objects that are identical except for size (i.e., small, medium, and large), a three-column Sorting Mat (see page 50), and Label Cards (see page 53). Put the label cards for "small," "medium," and "large" on the sorting mat. Mix up the objects, and place them in a basket near the sorting mat.

ACTIVITY Hand out a different type of object to each child. Have them take turns putting the objects on the mat, sorting them by size. When they are finished, ask them to compare the objects using the words *biggest*, *smallest*, *smaller than*, and *bigger than*. For hats, for example, ask the following questions:

- Which is the biggest hat?
- Which is the smallest hat?
- Which hat is smaller than this hat? (Point to the medium-sized hat.)
- Which hat is bigger than this hat?

Encourage the children to answer your questions in complete sentences.

EXTENSION Give two children pairs of miniatures to compare in size. Ask one child to use size words to compare his object to his partner's. He might say, for example, "My tree is taller than her tree."

Animal Babies

Children enjoy learning animal baby names.

SET UP   Display pairs of animals—an adult and a baby—for animals like the following: goat (kid), dog (puppy), cat (kitten), bear (cub), rabbit (bunny), duck (duckling), or sheep (lamb). In some cases, the adult male and female have special names as well. Examples are doe (female), buck (male), and fawn (baby); rooster (male), hen (female), and chick (baby); cow (female), bull (male), and calf (baby).

ACTIVITY   Have the children match the adult animal(s) with the baby and tell the names for each.

EXTENSION   Give each child or pair of children an animal family, and invite them to make up a story about the animals. They can act out their stories on story mats, if desired. For example, a child might act out a story about how a duckling gets lost and the mother duck searches for her. The story could be acted out on the At the Pond story mat. (See page 55.)

20 Questions

Not an easy game for young children, 20 Questions builds reasoning and language skills.

SET UP Use objects from several categories for this activity. For example, you might choose the four categories Insects, Zoo Animals, Clothes, and Tools. Mix up the objects, and spread them out on a felt workmat.

ACTIVITY Choose a secret object from the set on the workmat. Invite the children to take turns asking you questions that have "yes" or "no" answers until they are able to identify the object. For example, if your secret object is a ladybug, the children might ask the following questions:

- Is it a tool? (no)
- Is it something you wear? (no)
- Does it have legs? (yes)
- Does it have four legs? (no)
- Does it have six legs? (yes)
- Does it have wings? (yes)
- Does it bite or sting? (no)
- Is it red with black dots? (yes)

Help the children with vocabulary words and phrasing as needed. After each question, talk about what the answer means. Say, for example, "It is not a tool, so I know that it is not the saw or the screwdriver or the shovel." Or, if the answer is "yes," say, for example, "It has wings, so it could be a butterfly. It could be a bee. It could be a ladybug. If it has wings, it can't be an ant." Point to each object and physically separate out objects that are eliminated from contention.

EXTENSION If the children are experiencing difficulty with this activity, you can reverse roles at first. Have the children pick a secret object and then you ask "yes" or "no" questions that narrow down the possibilities. Verbalize your thinking process, explaining how the answers give you clues to the secret object.

Not Me!

This activity gives children practice with positive and negative sentences. It is also a great way to build vocabulary words.

SET UP Choose a category (e.g., Zoo Animals), and pass out an object to each child.

ACTIVITY Go around the group having each child say something about his or her object such as, "My animal has four legs." Children who have an object with the same characteristic say, "Me, too." Then they repeat the same sentence. Children who do not have the same characteristic say, "Not me," and then a sentence. A child's sentence might be, for example, "My animal does not have four legs."

Help the children verbalize their thinking as needed. For example, a child may know that an elephant has tusks but not know the word for them. The child can show you and the other children by pointing to the tusks on the object, and you can introduce the vocabulary word to everyone. Encourage the use of the word by having each child use the word in a sentence. For example, a child with a camel would say, "An elephant has tusks, but a camel does not have tusks."

EXTENSION Give each child a pair of objects and ask them to compare the two. Invite them to say one way that the animals are alike and one way that they are different. A child who has a raccoon and a frog, for example, might say the following:

Both animals have two eyes.
A raccoon has fur, and a frog does not have fur.

Riddles

It flies. It has a tail. No, it's not a flying squirrel! It's a kite.

SET UP   Place about ten objects on a felt workmat, all from one category or a mixture from several different categories.

ACTIVITY   Tell the children that you are thinking of an object and you want them to figure out what it is. Give clues in riddle form. Help the children with the vocabulary for each clue by pointing to an example on one of the objects. For example, you might display different kinds of vehicles (e.g., truck, boat, plane, car, bus, and train) and give the following clues:

- It has doors.
- It has windows.
- It has seats.
- It has tires.
- It has a motor.
- It has wings.
- What is it? (an airplane)

EXTENSION   Now let the children make up riddles for their classmates to solve.

Hear and Do

In this activity, the children listen to a sentence and then act it out.

SET UP   Use a story mat (see pages 55–62) and its related objects. Put the objects in a basket near the story mat.

ACTIVITY   Say a sentence involving one or more objects and some action. Ask a child to act out the sentence. Here are some examples:

- The frog jumped off the log into the pond.
- The bird flew from the nest in the tree to the edge of the pond.
- The rabbit started at the tree and hopped around the lake.

Tailor the sentence complexity to the language level of the children in the group.

EXTENSION   Pair up the children. Each pair of children can work with a different story mat and set of objects. Have them take turns saying a sentence and having their partner act it out.

Story Map

In this activity, the children learn about the four key elements of a story.

SET UP Have several felt story mats ready. (See pages 55–62.) Place story characters (miniature animals or people) in a basket. Make copies of the Story Map graphic organizer on page 54.

ACTIVITY Tell the children that the class will be creating a story today. Before they begin to tell their story, they will plan it out using a story map. Start by asking the children where they would like the story to take place. Explain that this is called the "setting." Have them pick a story mat for their setting. Write the name of the setting on the story map.

Next, show the children the basket of characters, and ask the children which ones they would like to have as the main characters in their story. Write the names of the miniatures in the "characters" box on the story map.

Now ask the children what problem the characters will face in the story. Decide on a problem and write it on the story map. Finally, ask the children how the problem will get solved in the story. Decide on a resolution, and write it on the story map.

Using the story map as a guide, have the children tell the story from beginning to end.

EXTENSION Repeat the activity on other days, picking a different set of characters, setting, problem, and solution.

Time for a Story

Children love dramatic play. Here they turn dramatic play into storytelling.

SET UP   Again, use the story mats and objects as described on pages 55–62. Put the objects for each story mat in a basket.

ACTIVITY   Give a story mat and basket of objects to each child. Have them use the objects to tell a story. The stories can involve all or some of the objects.

Give the children plenty of time to think through their stories. Then have the children take turns being storyteller, using the objects to dramatize the stories as they speak.

When the storyteller has finished, encourage the audience to applaud. What did they like best about the story? Did anything confuse them?

EXTENSION   Tape the stories, and listen to them later. Hearing their own voices on tape motivates children to perfect their articulation and pronunciation skills.

Blackline Masters

Ten in the Bed

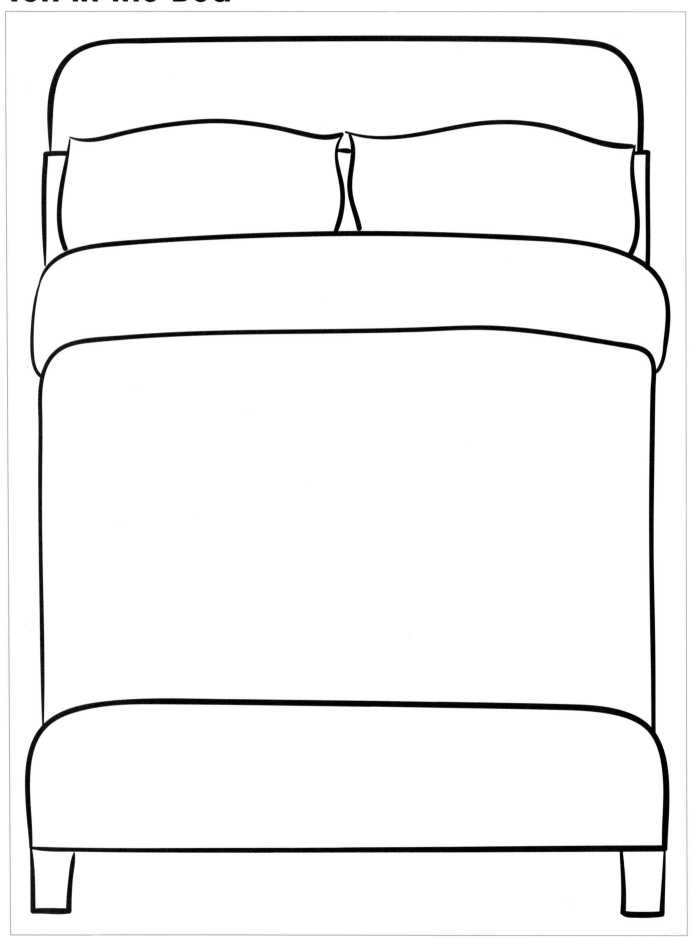

Paper Doll

Store Shelves

Sorting Mat (Two Columns)

Sorting Mat (Three Columns)

Realia: Making Language Real

Sorting Mat (Four Columns)

Sorting Mat (Five Columns)

Label Cards

land

sea

sky

zoo

farm

forest

sea

house

yes

no

circle

triangle

rectangle

oval

square

diamond

small

medium

large

Story Map

characters	setting
problem	**solution**

At the Pond

Realia: forest animals (e.g., frog, rabbit, duck, fox, owl, bird, skunk, bear, deer), nest, boat, picnic basket, blanket

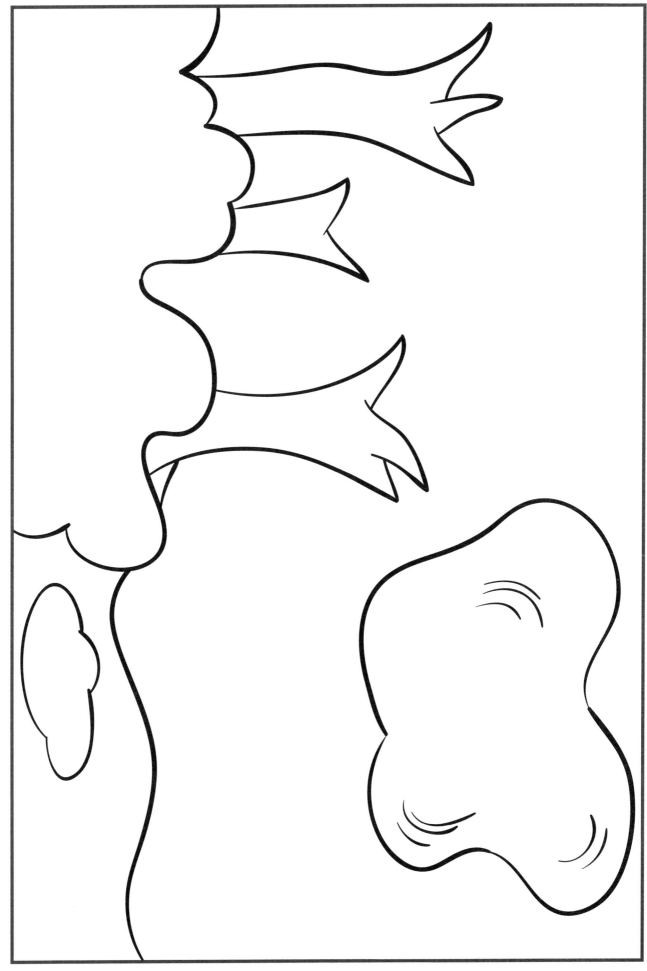

Under the Sea

Realia: sea creatures (e.g., shark, octopus, starfish, crab, turtle, lobster), sunken ship, treasure chest

In the Jungle

Realia: rainforest animals (e.g., monkey, parrot, tiger, crocodile, butterfly), log

Picnic in the Park
Realia: skateboard, kite, camera, food (e.g., apple, grapes, pizza, cake), ball, family (e.g., mother, father, sister, brother)

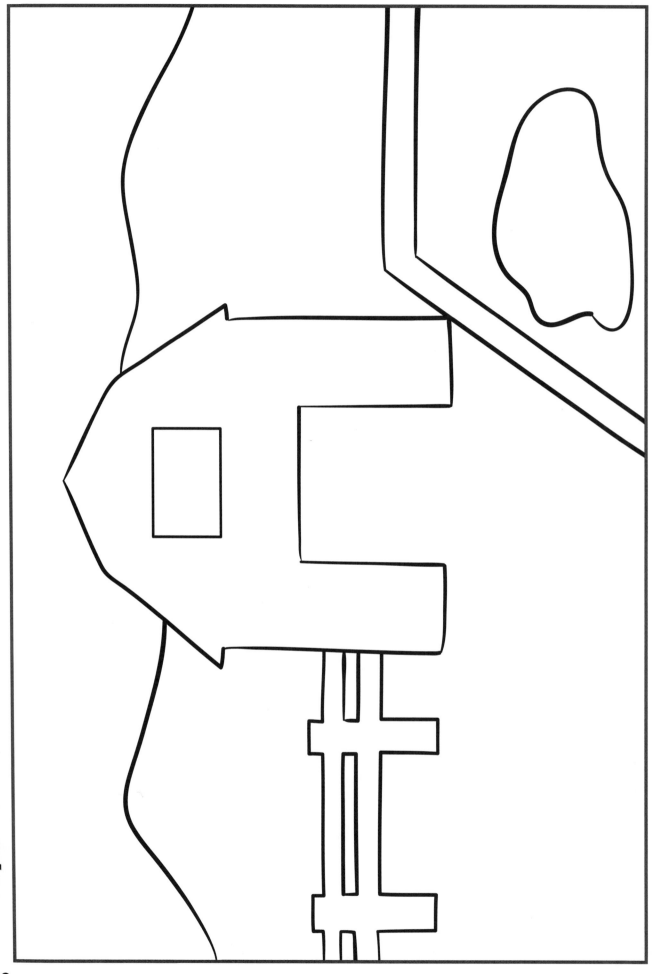

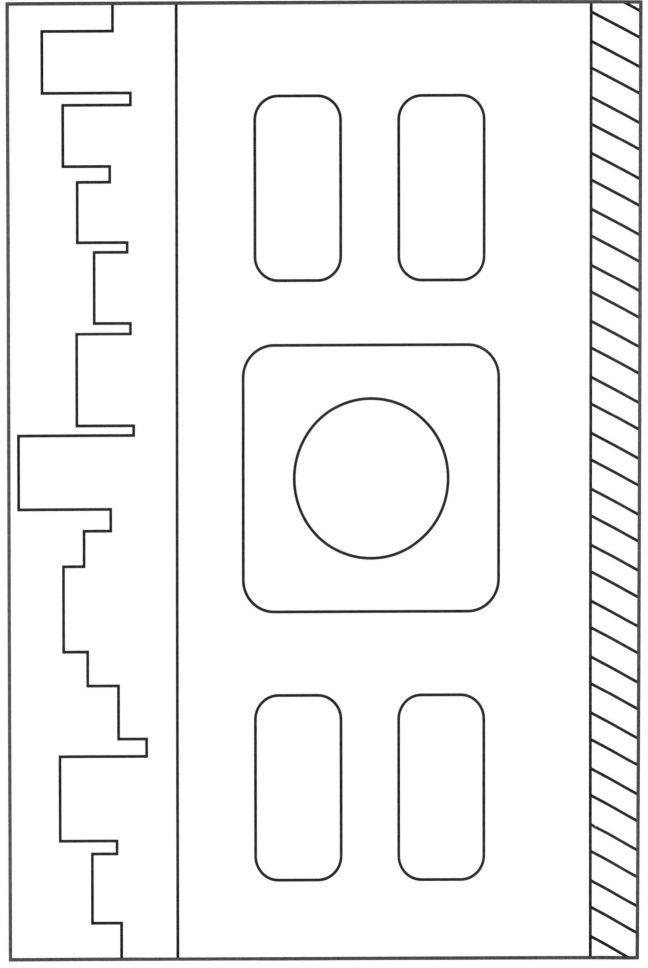

Around Town Realia: cars, airplane, helicopter, bus, motorcycle, bicycle, truck, signs

African Adventure Realia: lion, elephant, zebra, hippo, jeep, rocks